The Hay Cart

Geraldine McCaughrean
Illustrated by Mike Spoor

The farmer got down from the tractor. "There!" he said. "All the hay is cut, ready for winter."
The hay on his cart was piled up as high as a house.

"Tomorrow I will put the hay in the barn," said the farmer. He was very tired.
The farmer drove the tractor home, but he left the hay on top of the hill.

Along came Jilly the Horse.
She saw the big pile of hay.

"Mmm," said Jilly. "That looks good to eat."
So Jilly took a bite or two.

Along came two big rats and their babies. "Ah!" said the big rats. "This is just the place for a nest!"

Our babies will be snug in here."
The rats crept inside the hay.

Along came the cockerel, who liked to stand on the farm roof.
He saw the hay, piled up as high as a house, and he stood on that instead.
"Cock-a-doodle-do!"

Along came all the hens.
"That hay looks nice and soft," said the hens.
"What a good place to lay our eggs."
They flapped their wings and jumped up onto the hay.

Just then, it began to rain.
A little mouse crept inside the hay to keep dry.

Along came the cat. She sniffed.
"I smell rats," said the cat. "And I smell a mouse."

The cat jumped up onto the hay.
She began to scrabble in the hay.
"Where are those rats?" said the cat.
"And where is that mouse?"

She made such a scratching and a scrabbling that Shep the sheepdog heard her.

"Stop messing up the farmer's hay," yelled Shep. "I'm looking for rats," shouted the cat. "And I'm looking for a mouse."

"What!" yelled Shep. "There are rats in the hay, a mouse in the hay, and a cat in the hay? I must get them all out."
Shep jumped up onto the hay as well.

Then the cows came along.

"If we stand close to the cart, we can keep out of the rain," said the cows.

They stood next to the hay, but some of the cows were still in the rain.

"Let us stand next to the hay too," they said.

The cows all pushed each other.
They pushed the cart.
The cart rocked and went rolling down the hill.

"Oh no!" cried the mouse. "What's happening?"
"Oh no!" cried the rats. "Where are we going?"
The dog howled and the cat spat, and the rat babies bounced about.

"What'll we doodle-do?" screeched the cockerel.
"Cluck, cluck," said the hens.
   They all flapped their wings and jumped off.

The cart bumped and thumped down the hill. The animals all clung on tight to each other.

"Look out, Jilly!" shouted the cockerel.
"Oh no!" said Jilly. "I ate the hay and now the hay is cross. It's coming to get me!"

Bumpity-lumpity-thumpity-CRUMP!
Into the barn rolled the runaway hay.
There were animals everywhere.

Slowly everyone picked themselves up.
They looked at each other.
"Woof!" said Shep. "Miaow!" said the cat.
"Squeak, squeak, squeak!" said the mouse and the rats and all the little baby rats.

"That was fun," said Shep.
"Let's do it again!"